# US NAVY
# AIR WINGS

# US NAVY AIR WINGS

# AIR WINGS

## Flamboyant markings 1965-1975

# René J Francillon and Peter B Lewis

First published in 1988 by Osprey Publishing Limited
59 Grosvenor Street, London W1X 9DA
Member company of the George Philip Group

Reprinted summer 1989

© René J Françillon and Peter B Lewis

British Library Cataloguing in Publication Data

Françillon, René J. (René Jacquet), *1937*–
    US navy air wings.—(Osprey colour series)
    1. United States. navy. Military aircraft markings 1965–1975
    I. Title      II. Lewis, Peter B.
    358.4′183

ISBN 0-85045-870-6

Editor Dennis Baldry
Additional photography by Ken Buchanan, Jerry Edwards, Don J
Willis, Marvin Yates and the United States Navy
Designed by Paul Butters
Printed in Hong Kong

**Title pages** North American RA-5C of RVAH-13
at NAS Fallon on 22 May 1975. The aircraft
bears the AG tail code of Carrier Air Wing
Seven which was then assigned to the USS
*Independence* (CV-62). The bat insignia of
RVAH-13 is painted on the fuselage side, just
beneath the wing leading edge

**Front cover** The fabulous tail markings of VF-151,
displayed by one of their F-4Bs at NAS Miramar,
California on 16 March 1973

**Back cover** Identified by its dayglo tail, a DF-8F
Crusader drone basks on the ramp at Miramar
on 26 August 1967

**Right** Lt Randall H 'Duke' Cunningham, who
shot down five MiGs between 19 January 1972
and 10 May 1972 while serving with VF-96
aboard the USS *Constellation* (CVA-64), poses
on 16 March 1973 in front of the Top Gun A-4E
bearing his name

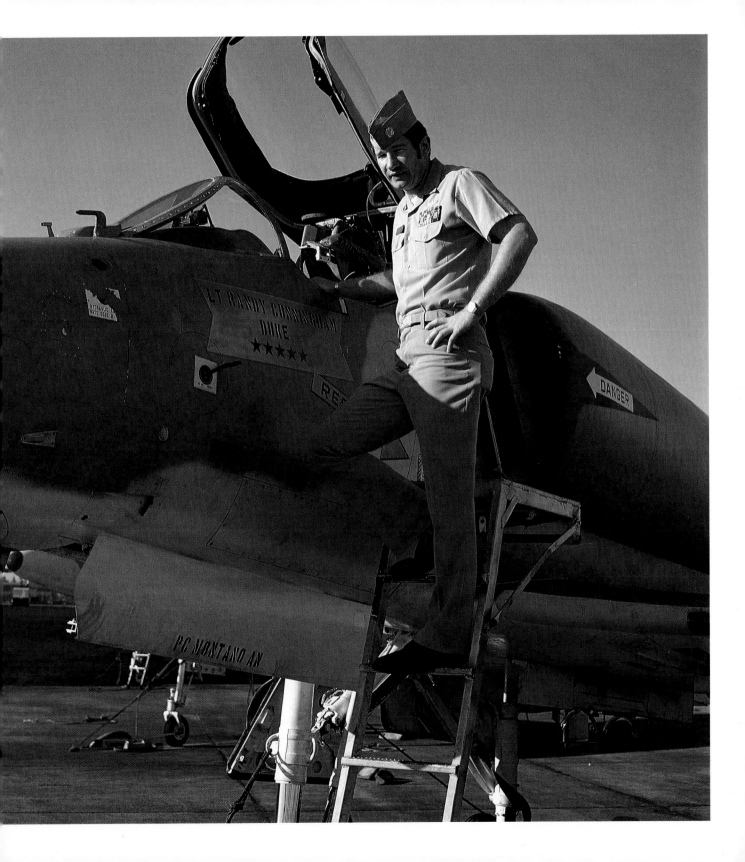

With the promulgation on 23 February 1955 of MIL-C-18263(AER), a new era began for Naval Aviation, as for the next 25 years carrier aircraft were to have unspectacular Light Gull Gray upper surfaces and gloss Insignia White under surfaces. Moreover, colourful squadron markings, which had begun to brighten naval aircraft after the Korean War, became the norm rather than the exception and in the process heightened esprit de corps, brought joy to aircraft enthusiasts, and boosted Kodak's profit. Even sustained combat operations in Southeast Asia did not lead to toning down these markings and the evaluation in 1965–66 of tactical camouflage for carrier aircraft remained inconclusive. In fact, the most colourful schemes were those carried in the early seventies by CAG aircraft. Unfortunately for Kodak and aviation enthusiasts, a new awareness of the ease with which brightly marked aircraft can be spotted and tracked by infrared sensors finally led to the progressive adoption of new TPS (Tactical Paint Schemes) in the early eighties.

This title in the growing Osprey Colour Series makes no pretence either to be an historical survey of camouflage and markings as applied to carrier aircraft of the US Navy during the 1965–1975 period or to be exhaustive. Rather, work on this photo book was begun by greying enthusiasts who, remembering with fondness the 'good old days' when photographing naval aircraft was fun, decided to share with younger enthusiasts their Kodachrome memories. You may not find in the midst of these 120 photographs one of your favourite aircraft or squadrons. We hope, however, that the splashes of colour on the following pages will help you forget for a moment the dullness of TPS and the drabness of subdued markings.

*René J Francillon & Peter B Lewis*
Vallejo, California, May 1988

Before it all began . . . Aircraft parked on the aft deck of the USS *Tarawa* (CVA-40) display three schemes in use during the early fifties. Most are in the Glossy Sea Blue finish adopted in 1944 for carrier aircraft and include Grumman F9F-5s from Carrier Air Group Ten (CVG-10)—with the identification Letter P and aircraft numbers in the 200 series—and CVG-4 (Letter F and 300 series numbers), and Grumman F9F-6s and Douglas AD-6s from CVG-3 (Letter K and, respectively, 100 series and 500 series numbers). The Cougar parked in front of the row on the starboard side is finished in the standard Blue Angels' colour (FS 15080) with Orange-Yellow NAVY but carries the side number 115, an unusual feature for a Blue Angels aircraft. The fifth aircraft on the port side, an F9F-5 from CVG-4, is in natural metal finish with clear protective coat as authorized in April 1952. (*Marvin Yates*)

# Contents

# Phabulous Tooms

**Left** With its ribbon drag chute deployed, an F-4J from the 'Freelancers' of VF-21 taxies back to the ramp at NAS Fallon on 21 July 1975. Even though it is located in northwest Nevada, some 240 miles from the ocean and at an elevation of almost 4000 feet, Fallon—'the carrier in the desert'—is the Naval Air Station to which Air Wings go to receive final training before deploying aboard carriers

**Overleaf** The 'Tomcatters' of VF-31 made only one deployment to the Gulf of Tonkin during the Southeast Asia War when they went aboard the USS *Saratoga* (CVA-60). VF-31 was on the line for 173 days between May 1972 and January 1973 and did not incur a single combat or operational loss while taking part in both *Linebacker I* and *Linebacker II*. This F-4J (BuNo 157293) photographed at NAS Fallon on 20 October 1973 bears a kill marking on its splitter plate, denoting that it was the aircraft in which Cdr Samuel C Flynn, Jr and Lt William H John shot down a MiG-21 on 21 June 1972

**Top left** BuNo 155863, an F-4J from VF-33, CVW-7, at NAS Fallon on 22 May 1975. The 'Tarsiers' also deployed only once to the Gulf of Tonkin, being aboard the USS *America* (CVA-66) as part of CVW-6 in 1968, and were also credited with the destruction of a MiG-21. The victors on 10 July 1968 were Lt Roy Cash, Jr and Lt Joseph E Kain, Jr

**Left** After deploying six times to the Gulf of Tonkin while flying F-8 Crusaders, VF-51 converted to Phantoms in 1971 prior to making two more wartime deployments. Before departing aboard the USS *Coral Sea* (CVA-43) for their first cruise with F-4Bs, the 'Screaming Eagles' adopted quite colourful and appropriate markings as shown by their CAG bird at NAS Miramar on 9 April 1971. VF-51 was credited with the destruction of two MiGs while flying F-8s

**Above** The 'Be-devilers' of VF-74 were part of CVW-8 when this Carrier Air Wing became the first to be assigned to the USS *Nimitz* (CVN-68). BuNo 157292, one of their F-4Js, was photographed at NAS Miramar in November 1975, six months after *Nimitz* had been commissioned

The 'Jolly Rogers' of VF-84 were aboard the USS *Independence* (CVA-62) when this LANT Fleet carrier made its only deployment to the Gulf of Tonkin. Armed with an AIM-9B and carrying MER racks and a ventral tank, BuNo 151478 is seen here on deck in August 1965. On the line for 100 days between June and November 1965, VF-84 lost three of its F-4Bs to North Vietnamese AAA. (*Jerry Edwards*)

**Above** BuNo 155772, an F-4J from VF-92, on final approach to NAS Miramar on 1 February 1975

**Right** Back from the Gulf of Tonkin for only eight months, VF-103 was again at NAS Fallon in October 1973 for yet another deployment aboard the USS *Saratoga* (CV-60). By then, however, Congress had mandated an end to US combat operations in Southeast Asia and VF-103 and the other CVW-3 squadrons were preparing to deploy to the Mediterranean

**Top right** VF-96 made eight wartime deployments during which its pilots and RIOs shot down ten enemy fighters. The first of these victories was obtained on 9 April 1965 while VF-96 was assigned to CVW-9 aboard the USS *Ranger* (CVA-61), the next was scored on 9 May 1968 when CVW-9 was aboard the USS *Enterprise* (CVAN-65), and the last eight were obtained during the first five months of 1972 when VF-96 and CVW-9 were aboard the USS *Constellation* (CVA-64)

An F-4J-40-MC from VF-114, with its refuelling probe extended in salute, at NAS Alameda on 24 September 1971. As part of CVW-11, the 'Aardvarks' made six wartime deployments, four with F-4Bs and two with F-4Js, aboard the USS *Kitty Hawk* (CVA-63). They shot down one Antonov An-2, two MiG-17s, and two MiG-21s

**Left** The tail markings applied to F-4Bs of the 'Sundowners' were among the most colourful. Those applied to their CAG bird, as seen at NAS Miramar on 11 October 1975, were even more spectacular

**Overleaf** Line-up of F-4Js from VF-142 on the ramp at NAS Miramar on 9 August 1974. Shore-based at NAS Oceana, the 'Ghostriders' were then assigned to CVW-8 for deployment aboard the USS *America* (CVA-66)

**Top left** The CAG bird of the 'Vigilantes' at NAS Miramar on 16 March 1973, less than two weeks after VF-151 had returned to NAS Miramar at the end of its last wartime deployment aboard the USS *Midway* (CVA-41). Note unusual application of CAG rainbow, in the colour of each of the squadrons assigned to CVW-5, beneath the wing tip

**Left** This F-4J from the 'Black Knights' of VF-154 displays less extensive, but nevertheless attractive, CAG markings as it sits on the ramp at NAS Miramar on 13 May 1975

**Above** On 12 January 1973 Lt Victor T Kovaleski and Lt (jg) James A Wise made the last kill of the Southeast Asia War, a MiG-21 brought down with an AIM-9 Sidewinder fired from this F-4B of VF-161. This MiG-killer from the 'Chargers', complete with victory marking on the splitter plate, was photographed at NAS Miramar on 16 March 1973

# Gunfighters & Photo Eights

Photographed on 26 August 1967, one day after the 'Checkertails' of VF-24 had returned to NAS Miramar at the end of a deployment aboard the USS *Bon Homme Richard* (CVA-31), BuNo 146992 is the F-8C which LCdr Robert J Kirkwood was flying on 21 July 1967 when he shot down a MiG-17; the aircraft was then coded NP 424. During the same cruise, from 26 January 1967 until 25 August 1967, VF-24 pilots claimed the destruction of three other MiGs and shared in the downing of another one, as evidenced by the $4\frac{1}{2}$ MiG silhouettes on the right ventral fin of NP 447

After deploying to the Gulf of Tonkin aboard the USS *Ticonderoga* (CVA-14) in 1964 and in 1965–66, the 'Screaming Eagles' of VF-51 transferred to the USS *Hancock* (CVA-19) for a 1967 war cruise lasting from 5 January until 22 July. During that cruise, one of their F-8Es was shot down by the North Vietnamese AAA and two others were lost in operational accidents

Photographed at NAS Miramar on 19 March 1970, this F-8J from VF-53 then had but a few days left in California before deploying aboard the USS *Bon Homme Richard* (CVA-31) for the sixth and last war cruise of the 'Iron Angels'

Assigned to CVW-16, VF-111 had an eventful cruise aboard the USS *Oriskany* (CVA-34) between May and November 1966. Two of its F-8Es were shot down by North Vietnamese AAA, one was shot down by a MiG, and one was lost in an operational accident. Three of its pilots were recovered but CAG, Captain W K Abbott, was taken POW on 5 September 1966 after he was hit by cannon fire from a MiG

**Top left** The 'Sundowners' of VF-111 made their last cruise in Crusaders in 1970 when they went to war aboard the USS *Shangri-La* (CVS-38). Their CAG F-8H, photographed at NAS Miramar on 19 March 1970, was then enjoying a few more days on the beach while the carrier was transiting around Cape Horn on her way from Mayport, Florida, to the Gulf of Tonkin

**Left** 'Double Nut', the CAG bird of VF-162, shares the ramp at NAS Miramar with other F-8Es from the 'Hunters', shortly after returning from a deployment aboard the USS *Oriskany* (CVA-34). During that cruise, the squadron's skipper, Cdr Richard M Bellinger, had been shot down by a MiG-17 on 14 July 1966 but had got his revenge by downing a MiG-21 on 9 October

**Above** In spite of appearances, the sailor standing beneath the wing of this F-8E from the 'Satan's Kittens' is not hosing down the right main tyre. Rather, the young man in 'Cracker Jack' white and 'Dixie Cup' hat tries to find something to look at to relieve boredom while standing by during an open house at NAS Los Alamitos in July 1967. VF-191 was then stateside between its first and second war cruises aboard the USS *Ticonderoga* (CVA-14). It had earlier deployed twice aboard the USS *Bon Homme Richard* (CVA-31) and later made four war cruises aboard the USS *Oriskany* (CVA-34)

**Overleaf** During operations in Southeast Asia, Crusader pilots were credited with the destruction of 18 MiGs. None of these victories, however, were obtained by the 'Red Lightnings' of VF-194. This attractively marked F-8J of VF-194 was photographed at NAS Miramar on 17 May 1975

**Above** VF-24, with red and black markings, and VF-211, with red and white markings, were the two fighter squadrons assigned to CVW-21 for five war cruises aboard the USS *Hancock* (CVA-19) between 1968 and 1973. Tails of their F-8Js are lined up at NAS Alameda before a final peacetime deployment in 1975. CVW-21 and *Hancock* were decommissioned respectively on 12 December 1975 and 31 January 1976

**Top right** After F-8s were phased out from Fleet squadrons, VFP-63 took over from VF-124 the responsibility for training F-8 pilots for the Reserve and RF-8 pilots for its own use and for assignment to two Reserve squadrons. This

resulted in 'fighter' F-8s being used by a reconnaissance squadron and in FIGHTERTOWN—the nickname of NAS Miramar—being painted on the rear fuselage of at least one F-8J in place of the usual carrier name

**Right** Beginning in 1964, RF-8A detachments from Marine Composite Reconnaissance Squadron One occasionally operated from carriers in the Gulf of Tonkin to supplement the small number of aircraft then available to VFP-63. This Photo Eight from VMCJ-1 seen shortly after trapping aboard the USS *Bon Homme Richard* (CVA-31) in the spring of 1965. (*Jerry Edwards*)

**Above** Until the summer of 1967, most VFP-63 detachments retained the squadron tail code PP on their RF-8As and RF-8Gs when they deployed aboard carriers. Thereafter, however, the appropriate Air Wing tail code—such as NF seen here on the tail of an RF-8G from VFP-63 Det 3 assigned to CVW-5 in early 1973—replaced the squadron code

**Left** During the Southeast Asia War, VFP-63 provided RF-8G detachments for operations aboard the smaller and older carriers. BuNo 144614 was one of the VFP-63 Det 34 aircraft working up with CVW-19 during the spring of 1970 in preparation for a deployment aboard *Oriskany*

BuNo 146858, an RF-8G from VFP-63 Det 1 assigned to CVW-21 for deployment aboard *Hancock* in the spring of 1973. Other RF-8Gs seen in the background carry the tail code NF, for VFP-63 Det 3 assigned to CVW-5, or the tail code PP, for aircraft not assigned to a carrier detachment

With the exception of a small CAG fin flash, this RF-8G from VFP-63 Det 3, with the tail code AC indicating its assignment to CVW-3 for service aboard the USS *Saratoga* (CV-60) in November 1975, has already lost most of the colours of yore. Soon drabness would settle in

# Bombing & Tanking

**Left** A Douglas A-1H from VA-196 moves into position prior to being launched from the USS *Bon Homme Richard* (CVA-31) off the coast of North Vietnam in the spring of 1965. (*Jerry Edwards*)

**Above** While equipped with Skyraiders, VA-25 made three war deployments, first aboard *Midway*, in 1965, and then aboard *Coral Sea*, in 1966–67 and 1967–68. For the first cruise aboard *Coral Sea*, the Skyraiders were coded NE, indicating that VA-25 was then assigned to CVW-2 as shown in this photograph taken at NAS Lemoore on 18 March 1967. For the next cruise, the last made by single-seat Skyraiders, the NL tail code of CVW-15 was applied

The 'Wild Aces' of VA-152 deployed three times aboard the USS *Oriskany* (CVA-34) during the early years of the Southeast Asia War. This line-up of A-1Hs was photographed at NAS Alameda after the aircraft had been off-loaded following the carrier's return to her homeport in San Francisco Bay on 31 January 1968

Based at NAS Alameda, VAW-13 maintained Detachment One at Cubi Point in the Philippines, where BuNo 132591 was photographed during the summer of 1965, to provide EA-1Fs for operations from carriers in the Gulf of Tonkin. Although old and slow, the EA-1Fs proved invaluable in detecting and jamming North Vietnamese radar installations

**Right** A 'Queer Spad', the ECM version of the Skyraider, aboard the USS *Independence* (CVA-62) during operations in the Gulf of Tonkin in the summer of 1965. This VAW-13 Det

One aircraft carries a black-painted experimental electronic device beneath its left wing. The device is said to have cost a pretty penny but to have been worthless . . .

**Overleaf** Gulf of Tonkin, summer of 1965. Aircraft parked on the forward deck of the USS *Independence* (CVA-62) include A-4Es from VA-72 and VA-86, an A-6A from VA-75, F-4Bs from VF-41 and VF-84, an EA-1F from VAW-13 Det One, an EA-3B from VQ-1, an RA-5C from RVAH-1, and an engineless A-3B from VAH-4 Det 62. (*Jerry Edwards*)

**Top left** While the USS *Hancock* (CVA-19) was making her way to the Gulf of Tonkin in August 1969, this KA-3B from VAH-10 Det 19 stopped over at NAS Barber's Point, Hawaii. VAH-10's sword fitted nicely on the refuelling probe of the Skywarrior

**Left** An EKA-3B from VAQ-131 at NAS Alameda on 23 October 1968, less than ten weeks before this squadron made its only war deployment— aboard the USS *Kitty Hawk* (CVA-63) from December 1968 until September 1969—before converting to EA-6Bs. The squadron's insignia, painted on the forward ECM fairing, is the same as that used earlier by the 'Fourrunners' of VAH-4, as VAQ-131 had been organized in November 1968 by redesignating VAH-4. Later, the 'Lancers' of VAQ-131 adopted a new insignia reflecting better the squadron's tactical electronic warfare mission

**Above** Photographed in the snow at NAS Oceana, Virginia, on 13 January 1973, this KA-3B from VAQ-130 Det One went aboard the USS *John F Kennedy* (CV-67) from April to December 1973 for a cruise to the North Atlantic and Mediterranean. (Ken Buchanan)

**These pages** An RA-3B from VAP-61 at NAS Alameda in June 1968. It is finished in the Light Gull Gray/Medium Gray/Sea Gray scheme specially adopted for night photo-reconnaissance operations over the Ho Chi Minh Trail

**Overleaf** The CAG bird of VA-23 at NAS China Lake on 16 March 1967 after returning from a deployment with CVW-2 aboard the USS *Coral Sea* (CVA-43) during which it flew 63 bombing sorties as evidenced by the tally on the right side of the nose

A-4Fs from VA-55, with black tail chevron, and
VA-164, with red tail chevron, at NAS Alameda
on 12 March 1975 before embarking aboard the
USS *Hancock* (CVA-19) before the last cruise of
Carrier Air Wing Twenty-One

**Right** A-4E from VA-72 and A-6E from VA-75
parked beneath vulture's row on the USS
*Independence* (CVA-62) during that carrier's
only war deployment to Southeast Asia in 1965
from 10 May until 13 December. (*Jerry
Edwards*)

Bearing the unofficial, but proudly worn, TONKIN
GULF YACHT CLUB patch just ahead of its mission
tally, this A-4B of VA-95 was photographed at
NAS Lemoore on 18 March 1967, four months
after the squadron had returned from its only
combat cruise prior to converting to Grumman
A-6As

The 'Roadrunners' of VA-144 were aboard the USS *Bon Homme Richard* (CVA-31) when that carrier last deployed to the Gulf of Tonkin in 1970. *Bonnie Dick* returned to Alameda on 12 November 1970 and was decommissioned on 2 July 1971. This A-4F was photographed at NAS Lemoore in April 1970, just before departing on this last cruise

**Overleaf** The 'Blue Tail Flies' of VA-153 got their nickname when one of their unpainted F9F-5s was fitted with the tail section of a dark blue Panther during operations off Korea aboard the USS *Princeton* (CVA-37) in 1953. This A-4C is seen here aboard the USS *Coral Sea* (CVA-43) during operations in the Gulf of Tonkin in April 1965. (*Don J Willis*)

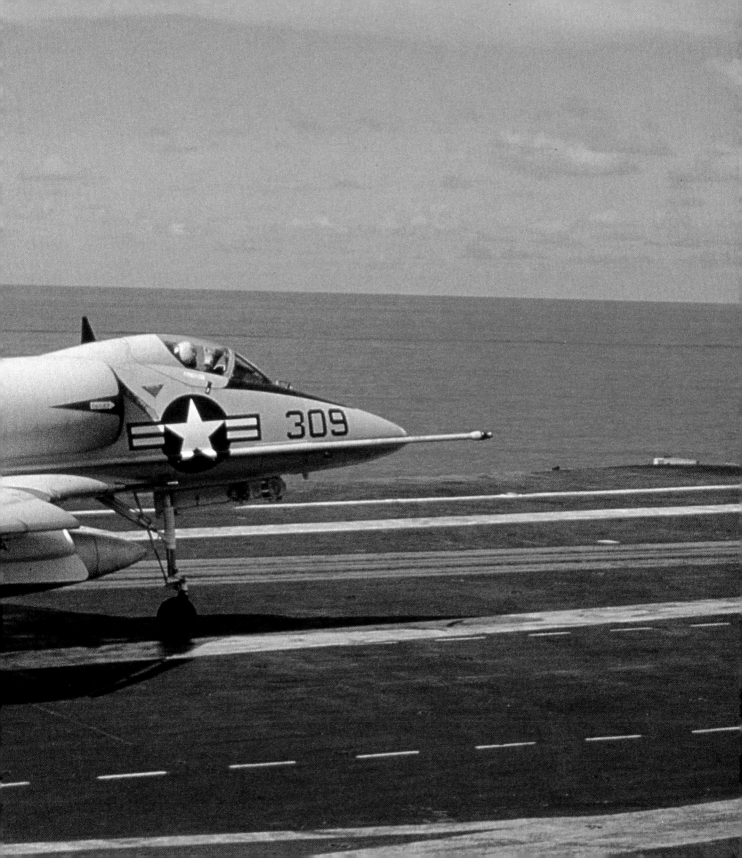

Photographed by the navigator of an A-3B from the 'Royal Rampants' of VAH-2, this quartet of A-4Es from the 'Silver Foxes' of VA-155 was returning from a mission over the North in April 1965. (*Don J Willis*)

LADY JESSIE, one of at least two Skyhawks known to have been named in honour of a benefactress who had a special fondness for the 'Ghost Riders' of VA-164. The top of Yerba Buena Island and the skyline of San Francisco can be seen beneath and behind this aircraft which was photographed at NAS Alameda on 12 March 1975

**Above** The 'Golden Dragons' of VA-192 were the first to deploy with A-4Fs, doing so aboard the USS *Ticonderoga* (CVA-14) on 27 December 1967. Their CAG bird was photographed five months earlier at NAS Los Alamitos

**Top right** The insignia of the 'Rampant Raiders' of VA-212 was inspired by the rampant lion on cans of *Coors* beer, an important fuel during R&R. During the Southeast Asia War, VA-212 deployed eight times to the Gulf of Tonkin, twice aboard *Hancock* with A-4Es, twice aboard *Bonnie Dick*, (first with A-4Es and then with A-4Fs), and again four times aboard *Hancock* with A-4Fs. BuNo 154973 was photographed at NAS Lemoore on 13 October 1974, 14 months after US combat operations in Southeast Asia had ended

**Right** Named HEAD SAVAGE, this RA-5C (BuNo 156632) was assigned in March 1974 to the skipper of the 'Savage Sons' of RVAH-5

With fleurs de lys as part of its tail markings,
this RA-5C belonged to RAVH-6 and was
photographed at NAS North Island on 17 May
1975, four before days the 'Fleurs' embarked
aboard the USS *Kitty Hawk* (CV-63) for a
WestPac deployment

**bove** The 'Peacemakers of the Fleet' began
their transition from A3D-2s to A3J-1s during the
ummer of 1961. RVAH-7 was re-equipped with
A-5Cs in late 1964 and then made two
eployments to the Gulf of Tonkin aboard
*nterprise*, one deployment to the Med aboard
*dependence*, a war cruise aboard
*onstellation* (with one of the aircraft taken on
at cruise being seen here at NAS Lemoore on
May 1969), one Med cruise aboard *Forrestal*,
he deployment to Vietnam aboard *Kitty Hawk*,
nother Med deployment again aboard

*Forrestal*, and finally two WestPac cruises
(aboard *Kitty Hawk* and *Ranger*) before being
decommissioned in 1979

**Overleaf** RVAH-9 was equipped with RA-5Cs
between 1964 and 1977. BuNo 146702 was
photographed at NAS Fallon on 22 March 1974,
four months before the 'Hoot Owls' embarked
aboard the USS *Independence* (CV-62) for their
eighth and penultimate deployment before being
decommissioned

This A-6A of the 'Knight Riders', photographed at NAS Alameda on 9 April 1972, had either been left behind or was about to be ferried as a replacement as VA-52 had deployed aboard the USS *Kitty Hawk* (CVA-63) on 17 February 1972 and as the carrier did not return to her homeport, North Island, until 28 November 1972

A brightly marked A-6E of the 'Tigers' of VA-65
at NAS Fallon on 22 March 1974. The Echo
version of the Intruder was too late to be used
during the Southeast Asia War

**Top left** A LANT Fleet Air Wing, with a Far Eastern flavour, in a Western locale . . . enough to get one's geography thoroughly confused! After deploying to Southeast Asia aboard the USS *Saratoga* (CV-60) in 1972–73, CVW-3 painted its AC code with an oriental flavour as displayed here on A-6As from VA-75 at NAS Fallon on 20 October 1973

**Left** Tanker-configured Intruder from the 'Green Lizards' of VA-95 at NAS Miramar on 9 August 1974. Serving along A-6As, this KA-6D deployed to WestPac aboard the USS *Coral Sea* (CVA-43) between 5 December 1974 and 2 July 1975 when CVW-15 took part in Operation *Eagle Pull*, the evacuation of Phnom Penh, Operation *Frequent Wind*, the evacuation of Saigon, and the rescue of the *Mayaguez*

**Above** Since September 1973 the USS *Midway* (CVA-41) and her Carrier Air Wing Five have been homeported in Japan. This brightly coloured tail belongs to a KA-6D from VA-115, one of the CVW-5 squadrons about to move to Japan

**Overleaf** Details of the appropriate tail markings featured on A-6As of the 'Swordsmen' of VA-145. Assigned to CVW-2 for deployment aboard the USS *Ranger* (CVA-61), this Intruder was photographed at NAS Miramar on 16 March 1974

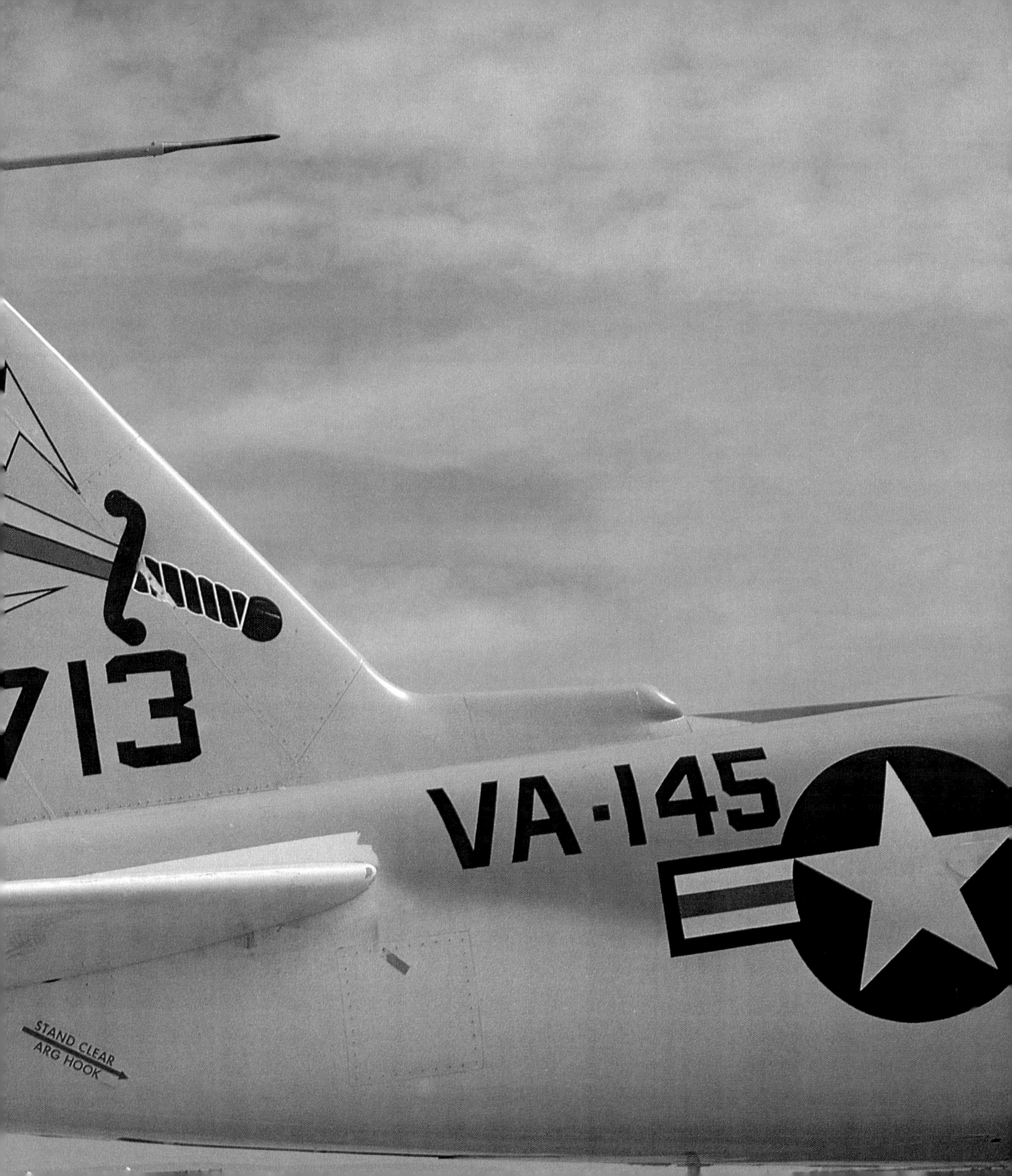
713
VA-145
STAND CLEAR
ARG HOOK

All-Weather Marine Attack Squadron 224 was assigned to CVW-15 for deployment aboard the USS *Coral Sea* (CVA-43) between 12 November 1971 and 17 July 1972. The 'Bengals' gained notoriety on 9 May 1972 when during Operation *Pocket Money* they mined the approaches to Haiphong Harbour

**Right** A KA-6D from VA-196, CVW-14, taxying at NAS Alameda on 13 September 1974. The tanker version of the Intruder was first deployed by the 'Arabs' of VA-115 when they went on the line in the Gulf of Tonkin in May 1971 aboard the USS *Midway* (CVA-41)

**Overleaf** The first EA-6B deployment to the Gulf of Tonkin was made by the 'Scorpions' of VAQ-132 aboard the USS *America* (CVA-66) beginning in June 1972. On that occasion, the squadron was part of CVW-8, whereas three years later, when BuNo 158806 was photographed at NAS Fallon, it was part of CVW-7 for deployment aboard the USS *Independence* (CV-62)

VAQ-137 was commissioned at NAS Whidbey Island in December 1973 as the seventh deployable TACELRON (Tactical Electronic Warfare Squadron) to be equipped with EA-6Bs. One of the 'Rooks' aircraft is seen here being hoisted aboard the USS *Enterprise* (CVN-75) at NAS Alameda on 10 October 1975

**Above** A-7E with the 'Kiss of Death' tail markings of VA-12. The squadron had earlier been known as the 'Flying Ubangis' when equipped with A-4s, but both this nickname and the 'Kiss of Death' markings were found offensive during the heyday of the Civil Rights Movement, forcing a nickname change to 'Clinchers'

**Top right** The *'Fighting Redcocks'* nickname of VA-22 has been more enduring and its markings are seen here on an A-7E photographed at NAS Lemoore on 12 October 1975. The aircraft partially seen on the right edge is an A-4S in Singaporean markings

**Right** Bearing CAG markings for deployment with CVW-2 aboard the USS *Ranger* (CV-61), this A-7E from 'the 'Fist of the Fleet' of VA-25 is loaded with blue practice bombs in preparation for a training sortie over the Fallon range on 21 July 1975

**Overleaf** Both the tail markings and the inscription on the drop tank proudly proclaim that this A-7E, photographed at NAS Lemoore on 22 October 1973, then belonged to the 'Royal Maces' of VA-27. Four months earlier this squadron had completed its last war cruise aboard *Enterprise*

**Above** Earlier equipped with A-7Bs, the 'Blue Blazers' of VA-93 switched to A-7As before moving to Japan in September 1973 as part of the forward-deployed CVW-5 for operations aboard the USS *Midway* (CVA-41)

**Top right** Until the much bemoaned advent of subdued markings, aircraft from the 'Stingers' of VA-113 always had some of the most attractive markings to be seen on naval aircraft. The tail of their CAG A-7E was photographed at NAS Alameda on 2 May 1974

**Right** After making four deployments in squadron strength to the Gulf of Tonkin in 1964–69 while embarked aboard the USS *Coral Sea* (CVA-43) and the USS *Constellation* (CVA-64), as well as providing a detachment for operations aboard the USS *Kearsarge* (CVS-33) during the early phase of the Southeast Asia War, the 'Blue Tail Flies' of VA-153 converted from Skyhawks to Corsair IIs. VA-113 then made three war cruises aboard the USS *Oriskany* (CVA-34). One of their A-7Bs is seen here at NAS Lemoore before the second of these deployments

**Left** During the early seventies, squadrons competed for the pride of having the most colourful CAG birds. This friendly competition is illustrated by the CAG birds from the 'Golden Dragons' of VA-192 and the 'Dambusters' of VA-195, the two A-7E squadrons assigned to CVW-11 for deployment aboard the USS *Kitty Hawk* (CVA-63) in November 1970

**Above** While equipped with A-7Bs, the 'Barn Owls' of VA-215 made one wartime deployment aboard *Enterprise*, in January–July 1969, and two wartime deployments aboard *Oriskany*, one between May and December 1971 and one between June 1972 and March 1973. BuNo 154454 was photographed at NAS Lemoore before the first deployment aboard *Oriskany*

# Stoofs, Willy Fudds & Hummers

**Left** BuNo 152840, an S-2E from VS-39, Replacement Carrier Anti-Submarine Warfare Air Group Seventy (RCVSG-70) being readied for launch off the angled deck of the USS *Essex* (CVS-9) in November 1967. (*USN*)

**Overleaf** Bearing the tail code AU of CVSG-56, this Grumman S-2G Tracker from VS-31 is seen flying over Narragansett Bay, off the coast of Rhode Island. (USN)

**Above** *Willy Fudd*, the only aircraft with its own umbrella . . . An E-1B from VAW-12 Det 62 has just recovered aboard the USS *Independence* (CVA-62) during operations in the Gulf of Tonkin in June 1965. (*Jerry Edwards*)

**Top right** Grumman E-1B from RVAW-110 Det 6 at NAS Lemoore on 13 October 1974 with the tail code NP of CVW-21. Based at NAS North Island, the RAG provided Tracer detachments for operations aboard the smaller carriers after the deployable Carrier Airborne Early Warning squadrons had converted to Hawkeyes

**Right** The 'Hunters' of VAW-111 sent more E-1B detachments to the Gulf of Tonkin than any other squadron. This E-1B from Det 31 was photographed at NAS North Island on 26 August 1967, the day after it had returned home at the end of a seven-month cruise aboard *Bonnie Dick*

**Above** A Grumman E-2A from VAW-115 at NAS Alameda on 23 October 1968, three days before the 'Liberty Bells' embarked aboard the USS *Ranger* (CVA-61) for their second deployment to the Gulf of Tonkin

**Top right** An E-2B from VAW-117 working up with CVW-3 at NAS Fallon on 22 May 1975

**Right** Hawkeyes have never been known for their beauty and seldom have had their lack of looks compensated by the application of colourful CAG markings. This E-2B from the 'Hummer Gators' of VAW-122, at NAS Fallon on 22 March 1974, proved to be an exception to this rule

# Trainers, Tests & Targets

During the mid to late sixties squadrons of the Naval Air Advanced Training Command made extensive use of Grumman TF-9Js prior to converting to TA-4Js. This aircraft from VT-26 was photographed at NAS Los Alamitos in July 1967

**Above** BuNo 155097, the beautifully maintained TA-4J assigned to Rear Admiral Burt Sheperd, Chief of Naval Air Training, framed against stormy skies at NAS Moffett Field on 10 October 1975

**Left** Throughout the Southeast Asia War, the Naval Ordnance Test Station at China Lake was one of the busiest centres developing weapons and weapons delivery tactics. In support of its RDT&E (Research, Development, Test and Evaluation) mission, China Lake used a variety of tactical aircraft including this A-4B photographed on 16 March 1967

**Top left** For almost a quarter of a century Grumman TS-2As, such as this aircraft from VT-31 seen at NAS North Island in July 1969, were used for multi-engined training. The first TS-2As had entered service with Advanced Training Unit 402 at NAS Kingsville in 1955 and the last were retired by VT-28 in 1974

**Top left** Used as a drone director, this China Lake DF-8F was a modified F-8A configured for remote control of QF-9F, QF-9G, BQM-34A, AQM-34B, and AQM-34C drone aircraft

**Left** This China Lake TF-10B had the nose radome of an A-4E grafted in place of the standard nose to test various Quick Reaction Capability (QRC) devices, notably Radar Homing and Warning (RHAW) systems

**Above** Drone director aircraft assigned to utility squadrons, such as this DF-8F of VU-7 at NAS Miramar on 16 May 1965, were among the most colourful naval aircraft of the period with their engine gray fuselage, orange yellow wings, and red tail surfaces

Even on an early smoggy morning at NAS Los
Alamitos in July 1967, there was no way of
missing this QF-9J drone

Built as an F9F-7 with a J33-A-16A engine, BuNo 130886 was later re-engined with a J48-P8 turbojet and redesignated F9F-6. Still later it was modified as an F9F-6K drone and then modernized as an F9F-6K2. This last designation was changed to QF-9G in September 1962. Seen here on display at China Lake on 16 March 1967, this green-tailed drone had obviously survived 17 remotely-controlled missions as evidenced by the tally on its nose

# CODs & Helos

**Left** Nose details of BuNo 146024, the COD aircraft assigned to the USS *Enterprise* (CVN-65) in December 1975. The 'triple nut' side number of this C-1A Trader has already been painted in bicentennial colours in preparation for the 200th anniversary of the United States which was celebrated in 1976

**Above** A pair of C-1As from VR-21 at Cubi Point in the Philippines during the summer of 1965. Throughout the duration of the Southeast Asia War, COD aircraft fulfilled a vital support role by shuttling personnel, mail, and urgently needed parts between shore bases and carriers on the line. (*Jerry Edwards*)

Although the C-2A was a much more capable COD, as it could carry heavier and larger items at greater speed and over longer distances than the C-1A could, the Navy could only procure 19 Greyhounds during the war years as available funds were then used in priority to procure combat aircraft and ordnance

**Left** Long before TPS (Tactical Paint Schemes) became the norm, Sea Kings used by HC-7 for combat SAR were finished in the subdued scheme illustrated by these two helos photographed at NAS North Island on 12 May 1975

**Overleaf** Helicopters were also used to shuttle personnel between ships operating in the Gulf of Tonkin. A crewman from VAW-13 Det One is hoisted from the fantail of the USS *Turner Joy* (DD-951), one of the two destroyers involved in the Gulf of Tonkin Incident in August 1964, for transfer to a carrier. (*Jerry Edwards*)

**Above** An UH-2C Seasprite from HC-1 Det 9 coming aboard the USS *Coral Sea* (CVA-43) during ORE (Operational Readiness Exercise) off the coast of California in August 1969. (*USN*)

**Top right** An extremely smart Kaman HH-2C Seasprite gunship ready for action at NAAS Ream Field, California on 12 May 1971. BuNo 150335 is from HC-7, a unit which specialized in combat rescue operations

**Right** An SH-3A ASW helicopter from HS-6 photographed at NAS Ream Field on 13 May 1971. Earlier, the 'Indians' of HS-6 had made four wartime deployments to the Gulf of Tonkin while assigned to CVSG-53 aboard the USS *Kearsarge* (CVS-33). During these deployments they flew both ASW and SAR sorties

# On deck & Below

The crowded aft deck of the USS *Oriskany* (CVA-34) as seen from a Seasprite from HC-1 Det 1 Unit G during operations in the Gulf of Tonkin in the summer of 1965. The aircraft are A-1Hs from VA-152, EA-1Fs from VAW-13 Det 1 Unit G, an A-3B from VAH-4 Det G, A-4Es from VA-163 and VA-164, E-1Bs from VAW-11 Det G, F-8Es from VF-162 and VMF(AW)-212, and an RF-8A from VFP-63 Det G. (*Jerry Edwards*)

**Left** Feeding the war. Munitions are being transferred from the USS *Pyro* (AE-24) during underway replenishment in the Gulf of Tonkin in the spring of 1965. (*Jerry Edwards*)

**Above** Four A-6As from the 'Sunday Punchers' of VA-75 parked beneath the island of the USS *Independence* (CVA-62) in July 1965. VA-75 was responsible for taking the Intruder into combat, doing so at the end of June 1965 when Carrier Air Wing Seven went on the line. Except for three aircraft which were destroyed in the premature detonation of their bombs during sorties between 14 and 24 July, VA-75 lost no aircraft and proved the A-6A to be an outstanding all-weather medium attack aircraft. (*Jerry Edwards*)

**Left** Looking aft from vulture's row, aircraft on the deck of the USS *Coral Sea* (CVA-43) during her September 1969 to July 1970 deployment include her C-1A COD, E-2As from VAW-116, A-6As from VA-35, and F-4Bs from VF-151 and VF-161. (*Jerry Edwards*)

**Above** A UH-2A from HU-1 Det 1 Unit E about to set down in the spring of 1965 as an F-8E from VF-191 is being spotted on the aft deck of the USS *Bon Homme Richard* (CVA-31). (*Jerry Edwards*)

Bombs aplenty. Budgetary restrictions in existence prior to America's involvement in the Southeast Asia War had resulted in a serious shortage of ordnance during the early years of the war. By 1970, when this photograph was taken aboard *Coral Sea*, this shortage had been remedied. The distinctive markings of the 'Sidewinders' of VA-86 can be seen on one of their A-7As. (*Jerry Edwards*)

**Right** Back from jamming North Vietnamese radar, a crew from VAW-13 Det One walks toward the island of the USS *Bon Homme Richard* (CVA-31). In spite of their age, 'Queer Spads' proved remarkably effective ECM platforms. (*Jerry Edwards*)

The hangar deck of *Bonnie Dick* shortly after CVA-31 had chopped to Task Force 77 on 12 May 1965. During 136 days on the line, Carrier Air Wing Nineteen lost 14 aircraft in combat (nine over the North and five over South Vietnam) and three in operational accidents. (*Jerry Edwards*)

The Wright R-3350-26WA powering the EA-1F loved oil, making engine maintenance work a rather messy chore. (*Jerry Edwards*)

While fuel is being transferred to *Coral Sea* during underway replenishment in the Gulf of Tonkin in the spring of 1970, a CH-46A has just lifted a hefty slung load from the aft deck of the fast combat support ship *Sacramento* (AOE-1). (*Jerry Edwards*)

Rounds of 20 mm ammo being belted for arming an A-1H from the *Wild Aces* of VA-152 aboard *Oriskany* in 1965. The Spad's four cannon were good weapons for forcing the enemy to keep their heads down during combat rescue operations. (*Jerry Edwards*)

**Top left** Hernia bar in hand, two Aviation Ordnancemen plot their course over 20 mm rounds while other red shirts tend to the needs of an A-1H from VA-152. (*Jerry Edwards*)

**Left** An F-4B from VA-96 launched off the angled deck of the USS *Ranger* (CVA-61) in August 1964 as the carrier was about to begin combat operations shortly after the Gulf of Tonkin Incident. Other aircraft on deck are A-4Cs from VA-94 and A-1Hs from VA-95. (*Jerry Edwards*)

**Above** A Crusader from VF-162 on *Oriskany* in the summer of 1965. During this combat cruise, their first, the 'Hunters' lost only one F-8E. Fortunately, after his aircraft had been set afire by the nearby explosion of a SAM during a mission on 5 October, Lt (jg) R F Adams, managed to reach the relative safety of the Gulf of Tonkin before ejecting. He was soon recovered by a Navy helo. (*Jerry Edwards*)

**Above** Sorry, we are full. From this angle, the deck of the USS *Oriskany* (CVA-34) appears to be too full for air operations to take place without first offloading some aircraft. However, this will not be necessary as skilled yellow shirts will soon restore order in the midst of this apparent chaos. (*Jerry Edwards*)

**Right** A tanker configured A-3B from VAH-4 Det 62 about to trap aboard *Indy* in August 1965. The aircraft has also flown bombing sorties as evidenced by the tally beneath the rear of the cockpit. (*Jerry Edwards*)

**Top right** You work on your tan whenever you can, wherever you can. Spending so much time in the confines of the ship without seeing the light of day or enjoying the smell of the sea, sailors are quite adept at taking advantage of rare opportunities to soak up the sun. While two Aviation Electronics Technicians do some maintenance work on an A-6A from VA-35, three other sailors have claimed the Intruder's right wing as their private place in the sun. (*Jerry Edwards*)

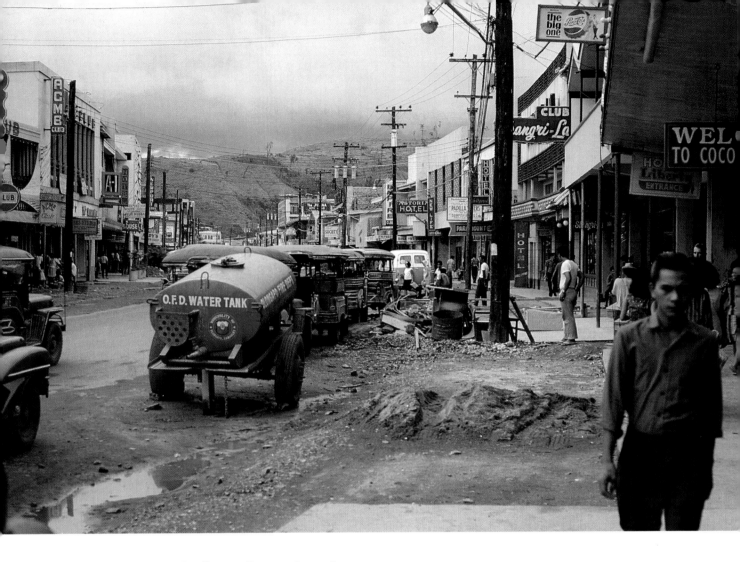

After weeks on the line, sailors and naval aviators looked forward to R&R in Hong Kong, Singapore, Sydney, or Yokosuka. However, more often than not the routine was broken by in-port periods in Subic Bay where all could find clean delight after long periods of confinement aboard ships with broken air conditioning and desalination systems. Oh, the joys of Olongapo . . . (*Jerry Edwards*)